OUR SCHOOL WORKERS

by Amy and Richard Hutchings
Photographs by Richard Hutchings

SCHOLASTIC INC.
New York   Toronto   London   Auckland   Sydney
Mexico City   New Delhi   Hong Kong

We would like to thank Jefferson Elementary School in New Rochelle, New York, and especially the principal, Mr. Kuhn, whose friendship we value and without whose support this book would not have happened.

We would also like to acknowledge the help of the teachers and staff of the Jefferson School, who graciously tolerated our impositions and interruptions. Thank you to all.

Last we would like to thank the parents and students who participated in this book, especially Joseph, our first day student and our wonderful young teacher, Beth.

This book is dedicated to our extraordinary editor and friend, Gina Shaw, for her encouragement.

And to Lena and Taylor for their first day of school.

— A.H. and R.H.

No part of this publication may be reproduced, or stored in a retrieval system, or transmitted in any form or by any means, electronic, mechanical, photocopying, recording, or otherwise, without written permission of the publisher. For information regarding permissions, write to Scholastic Inc., Attention: Permissions Department, 555 Broadway, New York, NY 10012.

ISBN 0-590-63840-8

Text copyright © 1999 by Amy and Richard Hutchings.
Illustrations copyright © 1999 by Richard Hutchings.
All rights reserved. Published by Scholastic Inc.
SCHOLASTIC, CARTWHEEL BOOKS and associated logos
are trademarks and/or registered trademarks of Scholastic Inc.

12 11 10 9 8 7 6 5 4 3 2 1   9/9 0/0 01 02 03 04

Printed in the U.S.A.   23
First printing, September 1999

Joseph is very excited *and* a little nervous. Today is his first day of school. Mom makes him his favorite breakfast—cereal and a glass of orange juice. Then they go outside together to wait for the school bus.

Here comes the bus!

"Good-bye, Mommy," Joseph calls from the bus steps.

"Good morning!" the bus driver says as he greets Joseph. "My name is Joseph, too. But everyone calls me Joe. Have a seat and I'll show you how to put on your seat belt. Every time you get on the bus, you must wear your seat belt."

Joe smiles as he drives the bus down the street.

There are lots of kids on the bus. Some are older and others are riding for the first time, just like Joseph. Soon Joe stops the bus and says to the children, "Here's your school! Wait for the aide to take you across the street."

Mrs. Bilic is a teacher's aide. She does many jobs to help the teachers in the school. "Good morning, children," she says. "Please line up behind me so that we can cross the street."

Mr. Hadani is the school crossing guard. He makes the cars stop. "Okay, Mrs. Bilic, the kids are clear to cross!" he shouts.

Mrs. Bilic leads the children into the school. She helps Joseph find his classroom. A smiling woman greets him at the door.

"Hi, Joseph!" she says. "I'm your teacher, Miss Corsell. Please find a seat." Miss Corsell also welcomes all of Joseph's new classmates.

Then she walks to the front of the room and says, "I know that today is the first day of school for all of you. And today is my first day of teaching school. I'm very excited to be here, but I'm also a little nervous!"

Joseph smiles. He knows that feeling!

Miss Corsell continues, "We have special visitors this morning."

Mr. Kuhn greets the class, "Welcome, everyone! My name is Mr. Kuhn and I'm your principal. My job is to make sure that the school runs smoothly and safely so that all of you can learn.

"Now I would like you to meet Mrs. Walton, the assistant principal. She helps me do my job and she works closely with the teachers. She solves problems and is in charge of the school when I'm not here."

Mrs. Walton welcomes the children to their new school.

When their guests leave, Miss Corsell says, "You just met some of the special people who work in our school. Now we're going to take a walk and meet some other people who work here. Let's line up!"

First stop—the library. The children walk into a sunny room filled with lots and lots of books. Mrs. Russert, the librarian, introduces herself. Then she tells the children, "You'll be visiting the library often throughout the school year. I'll read stories to you and help you find books that you might like to read." Joseph can't wait to start reading!

Next the class walks to the nurse's office. "Boys and girls," Miss Corsell says, "this is Ms. Kang, our school nurse. In the next few weeks, she'll test your eyesight and hearing. If you get hurt or feel sick during the year, you'll come here."

"I'll take good care of all of you," Ms. Kang adds.

The class goes downstairs to meet Mr. Sargeant, the custodian. "Mr. Sargeant does many jobs," explains Miss Corsell. "He cleans the halls and the classrooms, changes light bulbs, fixes broken windows, and makes sure the school is warm in the winter. You'll see Mr. Sargeant in many different places in the school."

Next Miss Corsell takes the class to visit the lunchroom. There she introduces the children to Ms. Ferrara. The lunchroom worker's job is to prepare and serve healthy food for lunch.

"Guess what?" says Ms. Ferrara. "It's lunchtime already!"

The children also meet Mr. Ponticello, the lunchroom aide. Mr. P. (that's what the kids call him) is the gym teacher, too. At lunchtime, though, he makes sure that all of the children clear off their trays and put their trash in the garbage or the recycling bin.

When everyone is finished, Mr. P. takes the boys and girls outside to play. On rainy, snowy, or very cold days, Mr. P. will bring the children to the auditorium after lunch and show them a movie. Joseph likes this idea!

As the children walk back to their classroom, they pass the main office. The school secretaries are busy at work. They have many responsibilities—they distribute the teachers' mail, they make copies on the photocopying machine, they type lots of information into their computers, and they keep a calendar of important dates.

Just as the children enter their classroom, the bell rings. It's the end of the first day of school! Joseph and his classmates have met many new people. Joseph likes his new school. He can't wait to come back tomorrow and get to know everyone better!

Do you know these people in your school?

school bus driver
teacher's aide
crossing guard
teacher
principal
assistant principal
librarian
school nurse
custodian
lunchroom worker
lunchroom aide
school secretary

Can you name other workers in your school?